DEDICATION

This guide is dedicated to my lovely wife, Ellen, who encouraged me with statements like: "(Sigh) I thought this was supposed to be funny."

Greetings! If you are reading this, then you must be concerned with surviving the end of the world. Or you could just have a morbid curiosity, the kind that makes you slow down and rubberneck by a really, bad wreck on the interstate.

Either way, you now hold in your hands the best advice you can grab when facing an end-of-the-world-as-we-know-it scenario.

Several scenarios are listed in this guide, with a handy "What to look for" section and a "What you will need" check list for each catastrophic, world-ending event. These scenarios are based on the major world religions' views of just what is going to happen when everything hits the fan. Some picture a violent, bone-crushing, flesh-burning episode. All their bloody, heart-rending, stomach-pumping details are included in this guide. Some see the end as a calm, peaceful transition to a better life. They are also included in this guide. Some religions do not have an end-of-the-world scenario. They are not included in this guide.

The purpose of this guide is to give you the best information available as the end approaches. This information will enable to you to assess the situation and respond in the best possible way with the correct tools at hand (often this includes a wet blanket). This statement is not a guarantee, though. If you end up making an ash of yourself, you will not be refunded the price of this guide.

The end of the world means a bad day for everyone. So please don't make it worse for your fellow survivors. Be nice to each other. Smile. Pat each other on the back and say bland statements like, "Well, it could have been worse."

What follows is an observation guide to determine which religion's end-of-the-world scenario is going down. It will guide you to the right chapter for all the information you will need. Good luck!

OBSERVATION GUIDE

- **Angel, single, blowing trumpet** (see **Islam**, p. 18)

- **Avatar on white horse** (see **Hinduism**, p. 35)

- **Beasts, hungry** (see **Christianity**, p. 7)

- **Blu-ray disk, Sony Picture's** *2012* (see **Mayans**, p. 48)

- **Boar, single** (see **Hinduism**, p. 35)

- **Camels, black, with cheerful shepherds** (see **Islam**, p. 18)

- **Cavalry, with weird horses** (see **Christianity**, p. 7)

- **Convenience store clerks become priests** (see **Judaism**, p. 26)

- **Crowds, large, dressed in white, holding palms** (see **Christianity**, p. 7)

- **Dwarf** (see **Hinduism**, p. 35)

- **Family, friends, dead, visiting** (see **Islam**, p. 18)

- **Gig, big, in Yemen** (see **Judaism**, p. 26)

- **Girl, slave, really pregnant** (see **Islam**, p. 18)

- **Goat herders, destitute, building large buildings** (see **Islam**, p. 18)

- **God of destruction with four arms** (see **Hinduism**, p. 35)

- **God of storms, drunk** (see **Hinduism**, p. 35)

- **Gods, demons at war** (see **Hinduism**, p. 35)

- **Earthquakes** (see **Christianity**, p. 7)

- **Fires, lots** (see **Christianity**, p. 7)

- **Hills, with wine and grain** (see **Judaism**, p. 26)

- **Horsemen, four** (see **Christianity**, p. 7)

- **Islands, moving** (see **Christianity**, p. 7)

- **Locusts, scary looking** (see **Christianity** p. 7)

- **Mahdi** (see **Islam** p. 18)

- **Maitreya, an advanced, spiritual being** (see **Buddhism**, p. 43)

- **Man-Lion** (see **Hinduism** p. 35)

- **Messiah in the clouds** (see **Christianity**, p. 7)

- **Meteor, falling in ocean** (see **Christianity**, p. 7)

- **Moon, blood colored** (see **Christianity**, p. 7)

- **Mountains, disappearing** (see **Islam**, p. 18)

- **Mountains, moving** (see **Christianity**, p. 7)

- **Neighbor, acting strangely** (see **Judaism**, p. 26)

- **Nothing (literally)** (see **Buddhism**, 43)

- **Peace, justice, common language** (see **Baha'i**, p. 44)

- **People, ignoring this end of the world scenario** (see **Mayans**, p. 48)

- **Plagues** (see **Christianity**, p. 7)

- **Plundering barbarians led by Satan** (see **Christianity,** p. 7; **Islam,** p. 18; **Judaism**, p. 26)

- **Rebellion** (see **Judaism**, p. 26)

- **Rulers, naked** (see **Islam**, p. 18)

- **Stars, falling out of the sky** (see **Christianity**, p. 7)

- **Symbolic ending** (see **Baha'i**, p. 44)

- **Temple, new** (see **Judaism**, p. 26)

- **Trumpets, various** (see **Christianity**, p. 7)

- **Vishnu, birth of** (see **Hinduism**, p. 35)

- **Warfare, among people** (see **Judaism**, p. 26)

- **Water, bad tasting** (see **Christianity**, p. 7)

- **Wheel of Dharma winding down** (see **Buddhism**, p. 43)

CHRISTIANITY

When the world ends in the Christian view, there will be no mistaking that you experienced a real, world-ending experience. There will be star-falls, mountains collapsing, weird, symbolic beasts dragging about, angels blasting overhead, and dead people mingling. If you miss all this, then either you are a really sound sleeper, or you wouldn't know the Apocalypse if it sat in your lap and said "mamma."

The end of the world, according to the Christian Bible's Book of Revelations, is suppose to happen 1000 years after Jesus' resurrection (Easter)[1]. But this number is symbolic, meaning lots of time. Otherwise, you wouldn't be reading this book in the 21st century now, would you?

<u>Things to watch for</u>:

- Plundering barbarians led by Satan;

- Messiah in the clouds;

- Various trumpets;

- Plagues;

- Earthquakes;

- Four symbolic guys on horses;

- Hungry beasts (including cats);

- Blood moon;

- Stars falling out of the sky;

- Mountains and islands moving about;

- Large crowds dressed in white, holding palms;

- Lots of fires;

- Meteor falling in the ocean;

- Really bad drinking water;

- Scary-looking locusts;

---

[1] *The New American Bible,* John 20 and footnotes, page 1245

- 100,000 soldiers on some really weird horses.

Things you will need:

- Binoculars (maybe);

- Up-to-date immunizations;

- Wild beast repellent (or cat food);

- Cardboard house (for earthquakes);

- Tree house;

- Flexible, long-distance calling plan;

- Wet blanket;

- A ticket with a number less than 144,001 from the DMV;

- Dry dock for your boat;

- White suit with palm;

- Stop watch or watch with a second hand or timer;

- Bottled water;

- Family pack-sized flying insect pesticide or repellant;

- Parthian repellent (whatever that is);

- Camera (maybe).

You will know when the end comes in Christianity. Initially, Satan will break out of his prison (where he was put there by the resurrected Christ) and gather up the Gog and Magog (see Judaism and Islam) and invade the earth and surround Jerusalem. Not to worry, though, fire from heaven will burn them up (ouch) and Satan will be thrown into a pool of fire and sulfur[2] (double ouch).

For starters, it will be pretty hard to miss the Messiah "coming amid the clouds and every eye will see him."[3] Even if you are inside the house, watching it on CNN, I'm sure you will

Satan being beaten up by Michael the Archangel.

see it. The network will probably cut away from its coverage of tax reform.

---

[2] Ibid, John 20:7-10

[3] Ibid, John 1:7

In case you missed that — which is doubtful - a series of seven disasters, seven trumpets blowing, and plagues caused by seven angels will probably catch your attention.[4] By the way, seven is actually symbolic, so don't start counting after the first disaster, blow and plague. Seven means "fullness and totality" in biblical literature.[5] So just because you counted to seven, it doesn't mean it's safe to leave the house.

There will also be four guys on horses, called by the real cool name,

Don't forget to feed the cats.

The Four Horsemen of the Apocalypse, which would be a real good name for a rock band. Again, they are also symbolic, so don't go looking in stables for the end of the world. They represent

---

[4] Ibd, John 6

[5] McKenzie, J. (1965). *Dictionary of the Bible.* Milwaukee: Bruce Publishing Co., p. 794

conquering power, war, famine and death.[6] The last guy, actually Death incarnate, apparently has a sidecar on his horse – or he is riding two to a saddle – because Hades comes along with him. Their job is to kill more than 25 percent of the world's population using sword, famine, plague and beasts.[7] I don't know how I would handle the first three, but as long as I feed my cats, the beasts are usually happy and napping. (Note to self: buy cat food.)

Now for those of you who live in a cave, or are watching American Idol, the next events might actually catch your notice since you haven't been paying attention. First, there is a big earthquake. Then, the sun will go black and the moon becomes like blood (This happened during a real cool eclipse I watched once). Then the stars will fall out of the sky. The sky itself will tear and curl up. All the mountains and islands will move to another place (I'm sorry; Puerto Rico is no longer in your local calling plan). And everyone will hide in caves and among mountain crags[8] (which will be a pretty mean feat considering that the mountains are moving

---

[6] *The New American Bible*, John 6:1-8

[7] Ibid, John 6:8

[8] Ibid, John 6:12-16

around at the time). What won't be touched this round of destruction will be land (sans mountains), sea and trees.[9] So, forget the mountains. Build a tree house!

Then the picking of those who are going to heaven begins. First, 144,000 will get their numbers called.[10] (It reminds me of the day I was waiting in line at the DMV. After waiting all that time, I had number 144,001.) Again, don't go counting. The number just symbolizes people from all the countries in the world.

Chances are, you won't make the first crowd, because they are a minority of people. The second crowd is bigger, so mingle with them. Put on a white robe, because everyone else is wearing one, and you don't want to stand out, and pick up your palm (the plant, not the hand). Every, countless one of them will be wearing white and holding palms.[11]

Then, things will get quiet. I'm not kidding. It will last for about 30 minutes[12]. Really.

---

[9] Ibid, John 7:3

[10] Ibid, John 7:4

[11] Ibid, John 7:9

[12] Ibid, John 8:1

But if you're still on earth and missed the white robe train, don't go out yet. It's like the eye of the hurricane warning. It may be quiet, but some really serious weirdness is going to go down in like 29 minutes and counting. Because at the end of that half hour (enough time to watch three episodes of *Sponge Bob Square Pants*), an angel will drop burning coals on the earth, causing thunder, rumblings, lightning and another earthquake.[13]

Now is the time to abandon the tree house, because seven angels will trumpet, bringing hail and fire mixed with blood, burning 33 percent of trees, land, grass (deploy the wet blanket); a giant meteor-looking object will fall in the sea, turning it into blood, killing 33 percent of the fish, whales, sharks and Nemo's mother, and wrecking a third of the ships[14] (your plans for dry dock better precede this).

Next comes a star named Wormwood (missed that one in astronomy class) that falls in the rivers and streams making a third of

---

[13] Ibid, John 8:5

[14] Ibid, John 8:8

the water bitter, causing people to die who drank from it.[15] Now would be a good time to break out the bottled water.

This will be followed by a succession of disasters: a third of the sun, moon and stars become black, and we lose a third of the day and night (sounds like Daylight Savings Time); a meteor punctures deep underground causing lots of smoke that darkens the sky; and then the locusts who come out of the smoke[16]. Well, they are more like locusts on steroids. They are wearing crowns, have human faces, women's hair, lion's teeth and iron breastplate-like chests (I think I dated someone like that.). These last are particular nasty because they can sting like scorpions and they will torture unbelievers for five months without killing them.[17] This, obviously, is when you will need the family pack-sized flying insect pesticide or repellant.

Then four angels will lead 200 million, really weird cavalry soldiers to kill a third of all the surviving people with their really bad breaths (fire, smoke, sulfur) and nasty, snake-like tails.[18] Of course,

---

[15] Ibid, John 8:10-11

[16] Ibid, John 9:3-6

[17] Ibid, John 9:3-10

[18] Ibid, John 9:13-19

don't take this literally. This is actually a rehash of a diabolical attack by the Parthians who were living east of the Euphrates River years ago.[19] Who knows, maybe they will be back. (What repels Parthians?)

The New Jerusalem! (Ignore the giant.)

Then the old world will pass away, and a new world will take its place, sans the sea.[20] A new, square Jerusalem will also come out of the sky and land on earth, and it will be really, really big. You should take pictures. Well, on second thought, who would you share them with? Anyone who is anyone saw the same thing and was also taking pictures, videos, etc. This city will be 1500 miles in length, width and height.[21] It will be the perfect cube! While there will be an angel

[19] Ibid, n. 9, 13-21, p. 1237

[20] Ibid, John 21

[21] Ibid, John 21:15

measuring it, don't get caught up in the excitement over the size. Again, this is a symbolic number. The measure 1500 miles is equal to 12,000 furlongs, which is 12 (the number of Apostles who will rule the new Jerusalem) X 1000 (meaning the immensity of Christians)[22]. You may get out your calculators, but take my word for it, it does equal 12,000. And since the symbolic 12 is in everything, that means the city is perfect![23] And it will be really pretty: pure gold with precious stones.[24] Ah, go ahead. Take that picture.

---

[22] Ibid, John 21, 16 footnote, p. 1246

[23] Ibid, John 21, 15-17 footnote, p. 1246

[24] Ibid, John 21

ISLAM

 blowing trumpet, exulting black camel shepherds and plunders similar to the Capital One advertisements are things to look for when the world comes to an end in Islamic style. A trumpet I don't have a problem with. I once took lessons. I could probably handle black camel shepherds, whether they are exulting or not. But plunders give me the willies. It reminds me of my brother-in-law.

Things to look for:

- An angel blowing a trumpet;

- Plunders coming through imaginary mountains;

- Large groups of people;

- Naked rulers;

- Black camels with cheerful shepherds;

- Largely pregnant slave girl;

- Destitute goat herders building Trump Towers;

- Long dead family and friends dropping by for a visit;

- Mahdi (if you're a Shi'ite).

<u>Things you will need</u>:

- Earmuffs or cotton;

- Capital One credit card;

- Muslim identity card;

- Water cannon ;

- Tarps;

- Camel pooper scooper;

- A team of OB/GYNs;

- A good building code;

- Air freshener;

- Wet blanket.

For starters, the Qur'an, the holy book of Islam, states that know no one knows the date of the end of the world (the Hour of Doom) except for God (Allā). But there are some signs to look for. All the action will begin with the blowing of the trumpet by the Angel Isrāfil. (Earmuffs or cotton will help.) When that happens, all the people will come together (look for flash crowds, ready the water cannon to disperse them), the heavens shall open up, and the mountains will vanish like they were a mirage.[25]

Other signs to look for include: barefooted, naked, deaf and dumb (ignorant and foolish persons) as the rulers of the earth (tarp them); the shepherds of black camels exulting in buildings (deploy the pooper scooper); one of the five things (wrapped) in the unseen (only known by God) (no clue here);[26] a slave-girl giving birth to her mistress and master; and barefooted (deploy the OB/GYN team), destitute goat-herds vying with one another in the construction of

---

[25] Ali, A. 1997). *The Meaning of The Holy Qur'an*. Beltsville, Maryland: Amana., pp. 1586-1587

[26] Kitab al-Iman (The Book of Faith), BOOK ONE, CHAPTER SEVEN. AVAILABLE ONLINE: www.iiu.edu.my/deed/hadith/muslim/001_smt.html

magnificent buildings (enforce strong building codes).[27] Some

seriously weird

stuff.

Beware of

the Gog and Magog!

They are apparently

several groups of

The plunders will destroy civilization as we now it. Wait a minute, what's that in the background?

unsavory, infidel (don't believe in Islam) plunders who will overrun

the faithful if one doesn't watch out. There is some barrier (a wall)

now holding them back, stretching from mountain to mountain. but

at the end of the world (Day of Doom), they will be let out and will

"swiftly swarm from every hill."[28] That will probably happen when

the mountains disappear like a mirage. So you might want to rethink

that retirement in a mountain top cabin. But don't leave home

without your Capital One credit card. Apparently barbarian plunders

respect this according to TV.

Christians will see a familiar face at the end of the world

amidst all these Quranic episodes: Jesus. Jesus will return on the last

---

[27] Ibid, book one, chapter one

[28] 'Ali, A., Surah 21:96

day in both Christianity and Islam. The Qur'an says Jesus is a prophet of God and not the last one (that honor goes to Muhammad). But Jesus is the prophet that will judge the end of the world, nonetheless. "And this (Jesus) shall be a sign (for the coming of) the Hour (of Judgment). Therefore have no doubt about the (Hour), but follow ye me; this is a straight way."[29]

However, if the Muslim way of the end of the world happens, it would do well to keep one's Christianity hidden. Apparently even Jesus doesn't like Christians.[30] So some sort of identification –

library card, driver's license, grocery store discount card, Social Security card, Green Stamps – from which can be inferred that you are some type of Muslim might be handy to carry around in your wallet, back pocket or purse in case the world suddenly goes sour. This, by the way, will all go

Dome of the Rock, Jerusalem: the place to be!

---

[29] Ibid, Surah 43:61

[30] Ibid, Surah 43:57

down in Jerusalem, probably near the third holiest site in Islam, the Dome of the Rock.

You will also meet your long dead friends, relatives and a lot of other people: anyone who was a good Muslim. They might be a little dusty and creaky – they have been in the ground for some time – but they're back (deploy the air freshener, if you wish, but you will be dead, too).[31] It is assumed that everyone will have their identification out and ready. And you can catch up on good times when you're standing in line with your luggage, waiting to be wanded and x-rayed, and…wait a second. I think that might be the wrong line. Ah…while you are waiting to be judged by Jesus and let into the Gardens of Paradise. Yes, that's it.

Paradise seems to be a nice place by all accounts: lofty mansions with flowing rivers below[32] and lots of gardens[33] as big as the heavens and earth combined.[34] One assumes there are no property taxes on this prime real estate. Whatever one wants, one

---

[31] Ibid, Surah 22:5-7

[32] Ibid, Surah 29:58

[33] Ibid, Surah 3:15

[34] Ibid, Surah 3:133

gets, there will be grapevines, a full cup of a favorite beverage and no arguing.[35] Sounds like Napa Valley.

Hell, of course, is just the opposite: a blazing fire[36], hotter than heat[37] (if that's possible) rejuvenating skin so the damned can continue to burn[38] (a wet blanket might be nice), the damned pleading to be destroyed[39], an evil bed[40] (I slept on one of those once), shame and no help.[41] And Satan will rule all this.[42] This may be best to avoid.

Another version of the end times is in the Shi'a tradition (they broke from the Sunnis, the majority of Muslims) that believes a Mahdi (guided one) will appear and lead everyone into an era of justice[43]. The Mahdi is not gone, just hidden. He could be standing

---

[35] Ibid, Surah 78:31-37

[36] Ibid, Surah 25:11

[37] Ibid, Surah 9:81

[38] Ibid, Surah 4:56

[39] Ibid, Surah 25:13

[40] Ibid, Surah 2:206

[41] Ibid, Surah 3:192

[42] Ibid, Surah 4: 120-121

[43] Hopfe, L. & Woodward, M. (2009). *Religions of the World, 11th ed.* New York: Vango, p. 365

behind you right now. (Did I make you look?) He could be in your

bedroom, the back seat of your car. You never know.

JUDAISM

I n Judaism, there actually won't be and end-of-the-world, fire and brimstone scenario, but a nice one, for Jews anyway. Jews will get back that hotly-contested city of Jerusalem forever, which will be a major bummer for the Palestinians. So maybe it is an end-of-the-world, fire and brimstone scenario for them.

Things to look for:

- Your neighbor acting strangely;

- A gig in Yemen;

- Rebellion, warfare, pestilence, famine and apostasy from God;

- Convenience store clerks become priests;

- A new temple;

- Wine and grain in the hills;

- Gog and Magog.

Things you will need:

- To be friends with your neighbor;

- A passport, visa and tickets to Yemen, then to Jerusalem;

- A small army and the Centers for Disease Control;

- A really good OB/GYN or midwife;

- A burial plot (or deed to one) really near Jerusalem;

- Lots of wine;

- A job in the diplomatic corps lined up.

The date and time of this new age apparently is a guarded secret among Jews. The prophets are not allowed to tell, and neither are the Jews when talking to idol worshippers.[44] So if you're not an idol worshipper, and you have a Jewish friend, perhaps you could take him or her out for a few drinks, maybe a few more, etc. and see what you discover. Just a thought. Don't accept the first excuse they might come up with, like a lengthy quote from the Talmud – "Whoever reckons the end, he shall have no share of the coming world" and "May the bones of those who reckon the end be blasted

---

[44] Epstein, J., ed. (1936). *The Babylonian Talmud: Kethuboth*. London: Soncino Press, p. 713

away."[45] Keep pressing. They will feel better about the whole thing after four or five glasses of wine.

Unlike in Christianity, the Messiah ("anointed one") who comes and reshapes the world in the model of Judaism is just an ordinary guy. He could be Bob, your neighbor (unless he told you otherwise while drunk). Or Otis, who runs the bowling alley. Maybe even Titus Andronicus, the pretentious clerk at the local convenience store. But he will have to be an observant Jew with a spirit of wisdom, insight, counsel, valor, devotion and reverence to God.[46] Okay, maybe he won't be Titus. Still, it could be anyone of your neighbors. And he might stand out, depending on the crowd you run with. DNA testing might help, because he is supposed to be descended from Jesse,[47] the father of King David, who founded Jerusalem as the original capital for the Hebrews. His ancestors will probably have not come over on the Mayflower.

But, interestingly enough, he may not show up at Jerusalem first. That might be his last stop in a multi-city tour ("If this is Saturday,

---

[45] Heschel, A. (2009). *Maimonides.* New York: Barnes & Noble, p. 94

[46] *JPS Hebrew-English Tanakh.* (2003). Philadelphia: The Jewish Publication Society, Isaiah 11:2.

[47] Ibid, Isaiah 11:1

this must be Jerusalem."). His first gig may be in Yemen, where he will show himself off.[48] Not all Jews believe that, but if tickets go on sale, maybe you better stand in line just in case.

Before he shows up, there will be suffering among the Jews. Because – as the imagery puts it – mother Zion (Jerusalem) will go through labor to give birth to the Messiah.[49] ("Push, push, breathe...") (A really good OBY/GYN or midwife would come in handy here.) The difference from a regular birth is that there will be rebellion, warfare, pestilence, famine and apostasy from God.[50] (So a really good OBY/GYN backed by the Center for Disease Control, the Red Cross, and a small army, might be in order).

The Messiah will do a number of things, so watch for them. For starters, he will reinstitute the Sanhedrin, the counselors, magistrates[51] and priests, who all became unemployed and had to get jobs at the local convenience store when the Romans destroyed the last Temple in Jerusalem in 70 A.D. (Okay, maybe it is Titus.) He

---

[48] Heschel, p. 99

[49] Epstein, p. 716

[50] Heschel, p. 92

[51] *JPS Hebrew-English Tanakh*, Isaiah 1:26

will also rebuild that Temple[52] and other destroyed cities.[53] (No word if my favorites, Sodom and Gomorrah, are included in that list.) And there will be mountains dripping with wine and hills waving with grain,[54] which is a good thing, because eating a lot of bread will help keep you awake during those all-night "wine-tastings."

The Temple, as it looked before (though much bigger).

If you are looking for a job in the diplomatic corps, now would be the time to apply. Because apparently all the other nations of the world are going to be asking advice from the messiah.[55] So, assumedly, he will have embassies in all countries. This means lots of jobs for ambassadors and other diplomatic types. You will be busy, going

---

[52] Ibid, Ezekiel 40

[53] Ibid, Amos, 9:14

[54] Ibid, Amos 9:13

[55] Ibid, Isaiah 2:4

back and forth with questions and answers: "Russia wants to know if vodka is allowed under kosher rules;" "Japan would like some specifications on that sword-to-plowshare proposal;" "The Koreas want to know what exactly is a pruning hook?"

One career move you may not want to take might be that of a funeral director or medical examiner. Because people will stop dying.[56] No business. In fact, all those you already buried will come to life.[57] And they will probably want their money back.

You may also not want to consider the education field. Everyone will know God's law and scriptures without having been told[58] (no classes, vocabulary drills, math problems, etc.)

And you certainly don't want to be a scholar. They will be persecuted.[59] Translated: no tenure.

---

[56] Ibid, Isaiah 25:8

[57] Ibid, Isaiah 26:19

[58] Ibid, Jeremiah 31:33-34

[59] Epstein, p. 728

There will also be no hunger, war, envy, fighting, and sensual pleasures. Goodness will flow toward everyone.[60] It will be basically an episode from Barney.

The place to be...buried: Jerusalem's cemetery.

All those in Zion (symbolic name for Jerusalem) will be saved from judgment, along with those really, really sorry for any sins they might have committed. So make sure you have a cemetery plot – or at least a deed to one – in the giant graveyard that circles Jerusalem (no one is allowed to actually be buried inside the city). This is the place to be when the Messiah comes. This is prime real estate. This is where the just will break through the soil and shamble... (Sorry, just can't get the zombie image out of my mind)...and rise up in Jerusalem.[61] Because Jerusalem is the place to be. Because everyone

---

[60] Hesche, p. 93

[61] Epstein, p. 720

else somewhere else is basically screwed. They will be crushed and killed.[62] That's got to hurt. (A one-time job for morticians.)

The latter, of course, are not going to be happy about this and they are going to rebel against God and the Messiah. Beware the Gog and Magog (see Islam)! Some rabbis interpret the second chapter of Psalms as a kind of a tag-team smack-down: God and Messiah vs. Gog and Magog.[63] This is definitely the heavy weight division.

Other than that, there really won't be any differences between the age of the Messiah and now.[64] So, since they are not

---

[62] *JPS Hebrew-English Tanakh*, Isaiah 1:27-28

[63] Epstein, J. ed. (1948). *The Babylonian Talmud: Berakoth*. London: Soncino press, p. 52

[64] Ibid, p. 215

excluded specifically, there still will be income tax forms to fill, electric bills to pay, rent or mortgage to cough up, and a job or school to drag oneself to. Maybe we can have a sit down with Titus and give some more input (bring the drinks!).

HINDUISM

 good thing about the Hindu view of the end of the world is if you miss it, you will get a second, or third, or fourth chance. This is because Hindus have a circular perspective of time. This means the end of everything happens over and over again. Still, each time everything ends it will be, to put it politely, horrific.

Things to look for:

- Human birth of Vishnu

- Demons and gods at war

- Man-Lion, Dwarf, Boar

- A drunken God of storms

- A nasty god of destruction with four arms (unlike the others, easy to spot)

- An avatar (not the large, blue type) on a white horse

Things you will need:

- To stay out of the way

- Binoculars

- Demon repellant

- Large alarm clock

- Sugar cubes

- A plant as a best friend

- A god-size cup of espresso

- Geritol and ex-lax

- A boat

- A wet blanket

- Fire and/or water insurance

There are actually several versions of the end of the world, according to Hinduism. Apparently not everyone can agree on what is just going to happen. In one scenario, time will lose its strength, Vishnu, the preserver god, is born human and the gods and demons – formerly friends – go to war against each other. The Man-Lion will fell the demon Hiranyakasipu (hope you didn't have any money on him) and Bali will be captured by the Dwarf (how embarrassing). Indra, the god of storms, will also kick some serious demon tush too. (Indra, by the way, is often drunk on Soma, an intoxicating drink from the plant of the same name.) And this war will somehow make the world better for humans.[65] So just stay out of the way and watch the action through your pair of binoculars. This battle is not supposed to include you. If you get too close, some of those demons will eat you.

The problem with this scenario is most Hindus do not believe it. These gods mentioned, like Indra, are no longer worshipped (they're just too old). It's time to make room for the new gods on the block.

One of these relatively new gods (younger than 4000 years old) is Shiva, the god of destruction and agricultural (he's a multi-tasker). He's a particularly nasty god who you do not want to meet in a dark alley. Case in point: Shiva's son, Ganesh, has an elephant head because his dad chopped off his first head in a fit of rage (where were the Department of Children and Families' case workers then?). Many Hindus believe Shiva, being the destruction specialist, will destroy the world. This makes sense. But since

[65] Dimmitt, C. & J. van Buitenan, eds. (1978). *Classical Hindu Mythology: A Reader in Sanscrit Purāṇas.* Philadelphia: Temple University Press, p. 67

Hindus have an idea of everything happening all over again, Shiva will also help recreate it.[66] Still, unlike the first scenario with Indra and Vishnu, no one survives Shiva's destructive fit. Shiva is also the god of agriculture, so if you have a fichus as a best friend to vouch for you, who knows? Still, to be safe, let's root for the old gods.

Shiva and family at the beach during happier times.

For you ladies waiting for a shining knight on a white horse, this end-time scenario is for you. Kalkin, the last avatar (messenger or manifestation of a Hindu god, not necessarily a 10-foot, blue alien in a 3D movie) will show up at the end of time.[67] This is where the sugar cubes (for the horse) may come in handy to endear you to both rider and equine.

There is also the equivalent of a cosmic oops in Hinduism. Brahma, the creator god, can destroy or create the world by thought.

[66] Esposito, J., et. al. (2009). *World Religions Today, 3rd ed.* New York: Oxford University Press, p. 324

[67] Dimmitt, p. 63

Just one thought. Hence the "oops" factor, particularly if he is having a bad day or is stuck in traffic. "In the dissolution of the world He alone remains awake. From that space He, assuredly, awakes this world, which is a mass of thought. It is thought by Him, and in Him it disappears."[68] A very large alarm clock might keep Brahma from being sidetracked, say, daydreaming the world away, and keep him awake enough to wake the world just in case he oops-es. A large cup of espresso may also keep him awake and focused.

A cup of espresso may also come in handy if a besotted Indra crosses your path.

And then there is the long, drawn out, everything-is-going-to-heck-in-a-hand basket end of the world scenario that you can hear on shuffleboard courts and bridge rooms. This usually comes from guys who have their pants pulled up to their chests and the luxury to complain about the government full time. ("Back when I was a kid, we didn't have air. And we were grateful. Not like these spoiled youngsters of today.") This scenario has us living in the last era before the destruction of everything, called the Kali Yuga, when

---

[68] Hume, R. (1975). *The Thirteen Principal Upanishads*. London: Oxford University Press, p. 435

priests will become unworthy, Hindu scripture will be forgotten, life spans decrease because of war and famine,[69] NBC will have problems with its evening lineup, cats will live with dogs, and the Postal Service will no longer deliver on Saturdays, etc. And then the world will be destroyed by a great flood. Or it will be destroyed by fire.[70] In this situation you will need the Geritol and ex-lax for the cranky, older people complaining all about this, a boat in case of flood and a wet blanket in case of fire.

[69] Esposito, p. 322

BUDDHISM

uddhism's view of the end of the world is (in my own words), "End of the World? Shmend of the World." Basically, don't worry, be happy (hmm, could be a song title). Empty yourself of all worry, possessions.[71]

What to look for:

- Nothing (literally);
- Wheel of Dharma winding down;
- An advanced, spiritual being named Maitreya.

Things you will need:

- A cat on which to meditate;
- A carefree, "who cares what happened to the car," attitude;
- A wet blanket (just for kicks).

Buddha taught that everything passes away[72], including the universe. You do, your friends, fluffy the rabbit, your car (don't I know that),

---

[70] Ibid

[71] Chah, A. (1993). "Our Real Home," *An Introduction to the Buddha and his Teachings.* Bercholz, S. & Kohn, S., eds. New York: Barnes & Noble, p. 90

etc. Don't become attached to anything, or else you will be disappointed. Presumably, this includes the world. Become one with nothing. Ommmmmmm. It is best to meditate on a cat. It has already achieved nothing between its ears.

So in a larger part of Buddhism really doesn't have an end-of-the-world-as-we-know-it scenario, because as far as Buddhists are concerned, the world as we know it is ending all the time anyway.

A more liberal branch of Buddhism, called Mahayana, has the closest to an ending than other Buddhist branches. One ultimately wants to become one with a universal Buddha, and therefore ceasing to exist as an individual.[73] There is also the idea that the current cosmic cycle or wheel of dharma (the time in which we are living) will eventually wind down and stop[74] (screech). But

---

[72] Oxtoby, W. & Amore, R., eds. (2010). *World Religions: Eastern Traditions.* Ontario: Oxford, p. 192

[73] Ibid, p. 206

[74] Ibid, p. 207

then it will be cranked up by a bodhisattva (a spiritually advanced being) named Maitreya and get spinning again. It's kind of like a party that winds down at 1 a.m., but gets a new life when someone discovers where the rest of the liquor is at about 1:30 a.m.

So the world, as we know it or don't know it, really doesn't end.

What is Buddha smiling at?
Well, actually...nothing.

BAHA'I

Well, the "end" has already happened and we're now living in the "end times." It's a good thing all of that is only symbolic. Even if it all did begin in a prison.

What to look for:

- Well, symbolic endings, I suppose.
- Peace, justice, everyone speaking the same language.

What you will need:

- Everything that Christianity, Islam and Judaism call for in their end of the world scenarios, except in symbolic form. Pictures of these items will probably suffice.
- Valid credit cards.
- Insect repellant (it will be Spring)

Baha'i believe their faith is a fulfillment of other faiths – Judaism, Christianity, Islam – and that all those end of the world as we know it scenarios mentioned in their Tanaks, Bibles and Qur'ans also apply to Baha'i.

Except, not really. Because it's all symbolic. The "Millennium" (translate as "the final chapter in our existence") actually began as early as 1917. God the Father had arrived in the form of the religion's second leader, Baha'u'llah.[75] This was predicted by the religion's founder, an Iranian Shi'ite Muslim, Mirza Ali Muhammad, in 1844, who was executed for even saying such a thing. Things didn't go well for "the Father," either: he spent the rest of his life in prison or under house arrest, and died in 1892 in Palestine (modern day Israel).[76] The next leader, Abdul Baha, was the Son of the Father (he actually was Baha'u'llah's son) and was Jesus. It was during his reign that the Millennium would occur in 1917.[77] The Son died a mere five years after this event.

So, if the "Millennium" came in 1917, you're probably asking yourself, "Where are all the stars falling out of the sky? How about the earthquakes (never mind recent events)? How about wars and

---

[75] Miller, W. (1974). *The Baha'i Faith: Its History and Teachings.* South Pasadena, Calif.: William Carey Library, p. 196

[76] Young, W. (2010). *The World's Religions: Worldviews and Contemporary Issues, 3rd ed.* Prentice Hall, p. 290

rumors of wars?" Well, okay. Some of these have happened, so forget I mentioned it. But what about those stars? Well, if you read the news or gossip magazines, how could you have missed them? Here are some "fallen stars:" Tiger Woods, O.J. Simpson, etc. Good thing our stars can rehabilitate themselves.

Alright, alright. Perhaps you missed the part about the end of the world being symbolic. To quote from Webster's dictionary, symbolic means:

1 a : using, employing, or exhibiting a symbol

1 b : consisting of or proceeding by means of symbols

2 : of, relating to, or constituting a symbol.

So, in Baha'i, you should look for a succession of new ages, not just one, final, end of everything event. Since each age has progressed naturally into the next one in the past, you could expect them to continue progressing naturally into the future. So valid credit cards will continue to be a must.

The Baha'i are optimists, so the world will actually get better in the last age.

---

[77] Miller, p. 196

This is how Abdul Baha describes it:

This period of time is the Promised Age, the assembling of the human race to the "Resurrection Day" and now is the great "Day of Judgment." Soon the whole world, as in springtime, will change its garb. "The turning and falling of the autumn leaves is past; the bleakness of the winter time is over. The new year hath appeared and the spiritual springtime is at hand. The black earth is becoming a verdant garden."[78]

There will be a "great peace" and people all over the world will fuse together into it, all speaking the same language, and there will be righteousness and justice on the earth.[79] Perhaps you could get the credit card companies to forgive your balance.

---

[78] *Baha'i World Faith: Selected Writings of Baha'u'llah and Abdul-Baha.* (1976). Wilmette, Ill.: Baha'i Publishing Trust, p. 352

[79] Hatcher, W. & Martin, J. (1985). *The Baha'i Faith.* San Francisco: Harper & Row, pp. 140-141

MAYANS

Those pesky Mayans! They seemed to have started this whole idea that the world was going to end soon. Supposedly when the current cosmic cycle ends, all are doomed.

But the problem with this scenario is that it is based on a mixture of ancient Mayan myth and astrology and few, if any, modern Mayans believe it.

Things to look for:

- Sale of the Blu-ray disk of Sony Picture's *2012*;

- People pretty much ignoring this end of the world scenario.

Things you will need:

- About $40 for the *2012* Blue-ray disk (unless you can get a discount);

- A large boat (maybe);

- Friendship with lots of spider monkeys.

The story making circles around the Internet, and now on Blu-ray, is that the Mayan Long Count calendar, written in glyphs (picture words) will have been on Dec. 20, 2012. The problem with this is that while Mayan dates correspond accurately to events in

The top of this Mayan temple won't even be safe if that flood comes

ancient times, they are more about the movement of planets, not history. The Mayan (in combination with the Aztec) calendar was used at least once before to predict the beginning of the end, well at least a great change: Aug. 16 or 17, 2010. Did you get the memo?

The Dresden Codex, which many of these prophets of doom seem to rely on, has eclipse tables that have cycles of 11,950 days.[80] While accurate for eclipses, the numbers become more symbolic in later years. For instance, the Mayans would plan attacks on neighboring kingdoms, and perform human sacrifices, based on the

---

[80] Coe, M. (2005). *The Maya, 7th ed.* London: Thames & Hudson, p. 226

The truth is in there: Mayan glyphs in Mexico.

position of the planets.[81] So it wasn't the Long Count calendar predicting events, it was events caused by the Mayans based on movement of planets in the Long Count calendar.

End-of-the-world-Mayan-want-to-bes also predict this end of the world scenario will involve a great flood. Mayan literature does mention a flood. One of the first attempts of the gods to create humans ended when all of these humans drowned in a great flood despite trying to climb on top of their houses (hmm, sounds familiar), on trees and into caves. Despite these people being wiped out, spider monkeys became their descendants.[82] Then people were created again.

Assuming this flood scene occurs at the end of the world, you may want to go biblical and build a big boat and put animals and your family and friends on it. Don't forget the poor spider monkeys. They probably had a difficult time during the first flood.

---

[81] Ibid, p. 228.

[82] Christenson, A. (2003). *Popol Vuh: The Sacred Book of the Maya*. New York: O Books, pp. 85-90

Made in the USA
Columbia, SC
20 August 2020

16770037R00031